Susie's Shed

Text by Ken Lancastle

Illustrations by Michael Roy

MCAC

Mechanical Contractors Association of Canada

BUILDING SMARTER TOGETHER

For information or permission requests,
please contact the publisher:

Mechanical Contractors Association of Canada
701-280 Albert St, Ottawa, ON K1P 5G8

ISBN: 978-1-0690647-0-7

Printed in Canada

Foreword

Thank you for your interest in Susie's Shed!!!

As a young girl I never dreamed or aspired to be in the construction industry. Only the males in my family were in the "business;" I was led to believe that construction was a boy's club, and unfortunately there was not a parent, teacher, or career councillor in my life that made me believe differently. Well girls, THAT COULDN'T BE FURTHER FROM THE TRUTH!

Susie's Shed was written to engage with younger generations and help debunk the myth that girls don't build. Construction is an amazing career choice for EVERYONE who enjoys working with their hands; the industry plays a vital role in the growth of our communities, and not least of all (attention parents!), careers in construction provide well-above average incomes, free of student loans.

This book was brought to you by Women in Mechanical Contracting (WiMC), an initiative of the Mechanical Contractors Association of Canada (MCAC) and all our provincial associations. But, girls, it is also important to note that career opportunities aren't limited to pipefitting, plumbing or welding. The entire construction industry is in need of electricians, carpenters, painters, drywallers, instrument technicians, and on and on and on. There is the perfect construction career out there awaiting each and every one of you. Dream it and it is possible!

To the parents, teachers, career councillors, and other influencers reading this book, know that our industry is a complex one that needs our best and our brightest. We need our GIRLS and our boys, and anyone that has an interest in building a better tomorrow for us all. Together we can break down barriers and create a more inclusive and welcoming industry for everyone.

To every child reading this book, know that your career can be anything you dream. Let your imagination take you on adventures and find what you love to do no matter what perceived obstacles stand in your way.

I love my job in construction and I hope you will too.

Judy-Lynn Mason
2024 Chair of WiMC

On a bright and sunny morning,
Susie was sitting on her floor,
Surrounded by toys, some books,
her dolls and lots more.

There were stuffies, and
stickers, and paper and glue,
But Susie just stared and said
"there is nothing to do."

"Mom!" Susie cried.
"I need you to stay."
"Or at least bring me
in to your work
for the day."

Her mom
simply smiled
as she went
out the door.
"Be good for
your Grandma.
And help
out with the
chores."

"Chores?" Susie thought.
"Mom can't be for real."
But then she came up with the most
marvelous idea.

Out in the backyard sat a dusty old shack,
A little bit of work could bring it all back.

"That's it," Susie shouted.
"I have a grand plan."

"My very own clubhouse for all of my friends."

Susie called her friend Ella,
who loved to do art, and asked her
to draw a design for a start.

Together they sketched
out all of their needs.
"We'll need a place we can play,
and a space we can read!"

Most importantly though was clean water to drink,

Including some drains for their new clubhouse sink.

So Susie sent Alex a message

so quick,
And Alex came running; she

knew just the trick.

The girls collected
a bowl and
a hose,

And rigged
up a system as
nice as a rose.

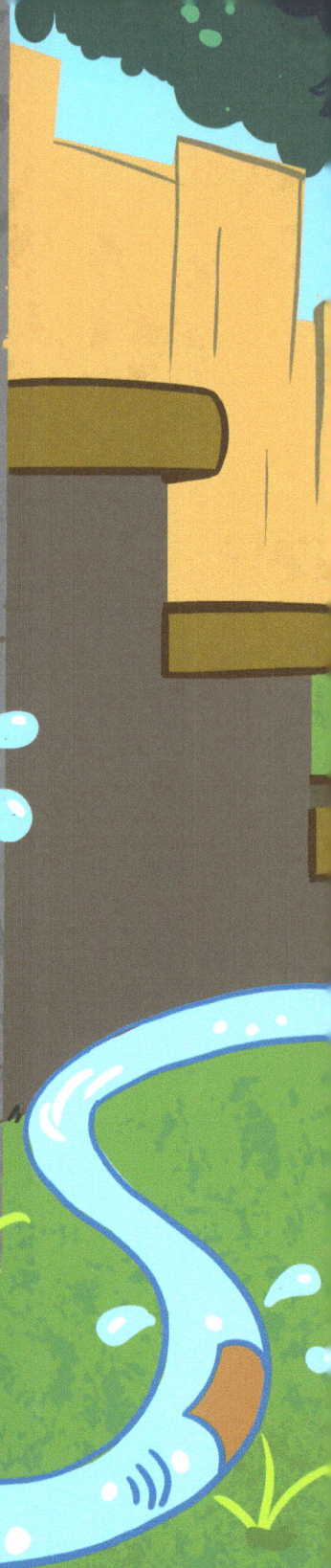

Alex turned on
the water,
and Susie switched
on the tap.

And water flowed to the
clubhouse as simple as that.

"It's perfect!" they cheered,
the clean water was ready.

But all that hard work made the
girls very sweaty.

The clubhouse was great in
almost every way,
But they needed something to
keep heat away.

"I've got it!" Susie yelled.
"We need boxes and glue."

And she drew out a plan and showed the girls what to do.

They each hunted down
the supplies they would need,

And wrote down the
measurements from
Point A to Point B.

This side up

Glue

They
glued boxes
together into a
long winding tunnel,
And rigged up a
system for the
cold air to funnel.

The girls danced
with joy as they felt the cold air,

The clubhouse was ready,
a place they could share.

Susie's Shed

Next
they
filled
the space
with pillows on the floor.

They added toys and books,
and made a space to adore.

When they sat down to play,
Susie heard her Mom at the front.

"Hurry please Mom!
Come see what we've done."

Her mom put down her stuff, including her hard hat,

And went to the backyard to see Susie's project.

The girls stood there proudly,
Their eyes filled with glee,

As Susie's mom smiled at all she could see.

Susie's Shed would not be possible
without the support of the mechanical
contracting community across Canada,
and our valued provincial/zone partners.

About the Author

Ken Lancastle has spent the better part of his professional career working with and promoting the construction industry, having worked in the construction association sector for close to two decades. He is a strong supporter of the incredible opportunities the construction industry provides, and believes more people should be exposed to the fantastic careers that are available for any individual, regardless of gender, race, or background. In his spare time, he can usually be found golfing, cycling, or, alongside his wife trying to keep up with their four young children.

About the Illustrator

Michael Roy grew up on a steady diet of Captain Crunch, drawing and Saturday morning cartoons, so it should come as no surprise that he ended up choosing a career in animation. For nearly 25 years Mike has worked as an animation director, creative director, art director, animator, character designer, storyboard artist and illustrator. As an illustrator and storyteller, Mike brings passion and dedication to his craft with a focus on character and visual storytelling. In his spare time you can find Mike spending time with his wife and son, competing in triathlons, racing bicycles of all kinds, enjoying photography and walks with his trusty great dane Blue.

Milton Keynes UK
Ingram Content Group UK Ltd.
UKHW050106071224
452013UK00022B/2